just for Kids

Publications International, Ltd.
Favorite Brand Name Recipes at www.fbnr.com

Microwave Cooking: Microwave ovens vary in wattage. Use the cooking times as guidelines and check for doneness before adding more time.

Preparation/Cooking Times: Preparation times are based on the approximate amount of time required to assemble the recipe before cooking, baking, chilling or serving. These times include preparation steps such as measuring, chopping and mixing. The fact that some preparations and cooking can be done simultaneously is taken into account. Preparation of optional ingredients and serving suggestions is not included.

Contents

Breakfast Bonanza

Rise and shine! Nothing gets kids moving in the morning like a hearty breakfast. Add a fun twist to the A.M. with these waffles, pancakes and other tasty sunrise specials.

Chocolate Chip Waffles

1 package DUNCAN HINES® Chocolate Chip Muffin Mix
¾ cup all-purpose flour
1 teaspoon baking powder
1¾ cups milk
2 eggs
5 tablespoons butter or margarine, melted
Confectioners' sugar (optional)

Preheat and lightly grease waffle iron according to manufacturer's directions.

Combine muffin mix, flour and baking powder in large bowl. Add milk, eggs and melted butter. Stir until moistened, about 50 strokes. Pour batter onto center grids of preheated waffle iron. Bake according to manufacturer's directions until golden brown. Remove baked waffle carefully with fork. Repeat with remaining batter. Dust lightly with sugar, if desired. Top with fresh fruit, syrup, grated chocolate or whipped cream, if desired.

Makes 10 to 12 waffles

Chocolate Chip Waffles

Breakfast Pizza

1 can (10 ounces) refrigerated biscuit dough
½ pound bacon slices
2 tablespoons butter or margarine
2 tablespoons all-purpose flour
¼ teaspoon salt
⅛ teaspoon black pepper
1½ cups milk
½ cup (2 ounces) shredded sharp Cheddar
    cheese
¼ cup sliced green onions
¼ cup chopped red bell pepper

Preheat oven to 350°F. Spray 13×9-inch baking dish with nonstick cooking spray.

Separate biscuit dough and arrange in rectangle on lightly floured surface. Roll into 14×10-inch rectangle. Place in prepared dish; pat edges up sides of dish. Bake 15 minutes. Remove from oven and set aside.

Meanwhile, place bacon in single layer in large skillet; cook over medium heat until crisp. Remove from skillet; drain on paper towels. Crumble and set aside.

Melt butter in medium saucepan over medium heat. Stir in flour, salt and black pepper until smooth. Gradually stir in milk; cook and stir until thickened. Stir in cheese until melted. Spread sauce evenly over baked crust. Arrange bacon, green onions and bell pepper over sauce.

Bake, uncovered, 20 minutes or until crust is golden brown.

Makes 6 servings

Breakfast Baskets

Silly Snacks

Move over, milk and cookies! Your kids will gobble up these fun and filling munchies. Refuel empty tummies with smoothies, snack mixes, dips and much more.

Pizza Snack Cups

1 can (12 ounces) refrigerated biscuits (10 biscuits)
½ pound ground beef
1 jar (14 ounces) RAGÚ® Pizza Quick® Sauce
½ cup shredded mozzarella cheese (about 2 ounces)

1. Preheat oven to 375°F. In 12-cup muffin pan, evenly press each biscuit in bottom and up side of each cup; chill until ready to fill.

2. In 10-inch skillet, brown ground beef over medium-high heat; drain. Stir in Ragú Pizza Quick Sauce and heat through.

3. Evenly spoon beef mixture into prepared muffin cups. Bake 15 minutes. Sprinkle with cheese and bake an additional 5 minutes or until cheese is melted and biscuits are golden. Let stand 5 minutes. Gently remove pizza cups from muffin pan and serve. *Makes 10 pizza cups*

Prep Time: 10 minutes
Cook Time: 25 minutes

Pizza Snack Cups

Super Nachos

12 large baked low-fat tortilla chips (about
    1½ ounces)
½ cup (2 ounces) shredded reduced-fat Cheddar
    cheese
¼ cup fat-free refried beans
2 tablespoons chunky salsa

1. Arrange chips in single layer on large microwavable plate. Sprinkle cheese evenly over chips.

2. Spoon beans over chips; top with salsa.

3. Microwave at MEDIUM (50%) 1½ minutes; rotate dish. Microwave 1 to 1½ minutes or until cheese is melted.

Makes 2 servings

Conventional Directions: Substitute foil-covered baking sheet for microwavable plate. Assemble nachos as directed on prepared baking sheet. Bake at 350°F 10 to 12 minutes or until cheese is melted.

Cook's Tip: For a single serving of nachos, arrange 6 large tortilla chips on microwavable plate; top with ¼ cup cheese, 2 tablespoons beans and 1 tablespoon salsa. Microwave at MEDIUM (50%) 1 minute; rotate dish. Continue to microwave 30 seconds to 1 minute or until cheese is melted.

Super Nachos

Super Spread Sandwich Stars

1 Red or Golden Delicious apple, peeled, cored
    and coarsely chopped
1 cup roasted peanuts
⅓ cup honey
1 tablespoon lemon juice
1 teaspoon ground cinnamon
    Sliced sandwich bread

For Super Spread, place chopped apple, peanuts, honey, lemon juice and cinnamon in food processor or blender. Pulse food processor several times until ingredients start to blend, occasionally scraping down the sides with rubber spatula. Process 1 to 2 minutes until mixture is smooth and spreadable.

For Sandwich Stars, use butter knife to spread about 1 tablespoon Super Spread on 2 slices of bread. Stack them together, spread side up. Top with third slice bread. Place cookie cutter on top of sandwich; press down firmly and evenly. Leaving cookie cutter in place, remove excess trimmings with your fingers or a butter knife. Remove cookie cutter.

Makes 1¼ cups spread (enough for about 10 sandwiches)

Favorite recipe from **Texas Peanut Producers Board**

Super Spread Sandwich Stars

Creamy Taco Dip

1 pound (16 ounces) VELVEETA® Pasteurized
   Prepared Cheese Product, cut up
1 container (16 ounces) BREAKSTONE'S® or
   KNUDSEN® Sour Cream
1 package (1¼ ounces) TACO BELL® HOME
   ORIGINALS™ Taco Seasoning Mix

Microwave all ingredients in 2-quart microwavable bowl on HIGH 5
minutes or until Velveeta is melted, stirring after 3 minutes. Serve hot
or cold with corn chips or tortilla chips.   *Makes 3½ cups*

Prep Time: 5 minutes
Microwave Time: 5 minutes

Tuna 'n' Celery Sticks

   4 ounces cream cheese, softened
   3 tablespoons plain yogurt or mayonnaise
1½ teaspoons dried basil
   1 can (12 ounces) STARKIST® Solid White or
      Chunk Light Tuna, drained and flaked
   ½ cup finely grated carrot or zucchini
   ½ cup finely shredded Cheddar cheese
   2 teaspoons instant minced onion
  10 to 12 celery stalks, cleaned and strings
      removed

In large bowl, mix together cream cheese, yogurt and basil until
smooth. Add tuna, carrot, Cheddar cheese and onion; mix well.
Spread mixture into celery stalks; cut into fourths.
                              Makes 40 servings

Prep Time: 10 minutes

Creamy Taco Dip

Purple Cow Jumped Over the Moon

3 cups vanilla nonfat frozen yogurt
1 cup reduced-fat (2%) milk
½ cup thawed frozen grape juice concentrate
(undiluted)
1½ teaspoons lemon juice

Place yogurt, milk, grape juice concentrate and lemon juice in food processor or blender container; process until smooth. Serve immediately. *Makes 8 (½-cup) servings*

Razzmatazz Shake: Place 1 quart vanilla nonfat frozen yogurt, 1 cup vanilla nonfat yogurt and ¼ cup chocolate syrup in food processor or blender container; process until smooth. Pour ½ of mixture evenly into 12 glasses; top with ½ of (12-ounce) can root beer. Fill glasses equally with remaining yogurt mixture; top with remaining root beer. Makes 12 (⅔-cup) servings.

Sunshine Shake: Place 1 quart vanilla nonfat frozen yogurt, 1⅓ cups orange juice, 1 cup fresh or thawed frozen raspberries and 1 teaspoon sugar in food processor or blender container; process until smooth. Pour into 10 glasses; sprinkle with ground nutmeg. *Makes 10 (½-cup) servings.*

Orange Smoothies

1 cup fat-free vanilla ice cream or fat-free vanilla
frozen yogurt
¾ cup low-fat (1%) milk
¼ cup frozen orange juice concentrate

1. Combine ice cream, milk and orange juice concentrate in food processor or blender; process until smooth.

2. Pour mixture into 2 glasses; garnish as desired. Serve immediately. *Makes 2 servings*

Purple Cow Jumped Over the Moon

Super Suppers

Cook up some fun for dinner tonight! Whether it's pizza or pasta, sandwiches or sides, the whole family will love these recipes (and the kids might even eat their broccoli).

Hot Diggity Dots & Twisters

⅔ cup milk
2 tablespoons margarine or butter
1 (4.8-ounce) package PASTA RONI® Four Cheese Flavor with Corkscrew Pasta
1½ cups frozen peas
4 hot dogs, cut into ½-inch pieces
2 teaspoons mustard

1. In large saucepan, bring 1¼ cups water, milk and margarine just to a boil.

2. Stir in pasta, peas and Special Seasonings; return to a boil. Reduce heat to medium. Gently boil uncovered, 7 to 8 minutes or until pasta is tender, stirring occasionally.

3. Stir in hot dogs and mustard. Let stand 3 to 5 minutes before serving.
Makes 4 servings

Prep Time: 5 minutes
Cook Time: 15 minutes

Hot Diggity Dots & Twisters

Sausage Cheeseburger Pizza

1 pound BOB EVANS® Original Recipe Roll
   Sausage
1 (12-inch) prepared pizza shell
½ cup yellow mustard
2 cups (8 ounces) shredded mozzarella cheese
½ cup chopped onion
15 dill pickle slices
¾ cup (3 ounces) shredded Cheddar cheese

Preheat oven to 425°F. Crumble and cook sausage in medium skillet until browned; drain well on paper towels. Place pizza shell on lightly greased 12-inch pizza pan or baking sheet. Spread mustard over shell; top with mozzarella cheese, sausage and onion. Place pickle slices evenly on top; sprinkle with Cheddar cheese. Bake 12 minutes or until crust is cooked through and cheese is bubbly. Cut into thin wedges or squares and serve hot. Refrigerate leftovers.

Makes about 8 servings

Green Beans Orange

1 pound fresh *or* 2 (9-ounce) packages frozen
   whole green beans
¼ cup SMUCKER'S® Low Sugar Orange
   Marmalade
1 teaspoon lemon juice

Cut ends off green beans; wash. Cover and cook in a small amount of boiling salted water until tender-crisp, about 5 minutes. Drain. (Or cook frozen green beans according to package directions; drain.)

Add marmalade and lemon juice. Cook and gently stir until beans are coated and hot.

Makes 6 servings

Sausage Cheeseburger Pizza

Amigo Pita Pocket Sandwiches

1 pound ground turkey
1 can (7 ounces) whole kernel corn, drained
1 can (6 ounces) tomato paste
½ cup water
½ cup chopped green bell pepper
1 package (1.0 ounce) LAWRY'S® Taco Spices
    & Seasonings
8 pita breads
    Curly lettuce leaves
    Shredded cheddar cheese

In large skillet, brown ground turkey until no longer pink; drain fat. Add corn, tomato paste, water, green pepper and Taco Spices & Seasonings; mix well. Bring to a boil over medium-high heat; reduce heat to low and cook, uncovered, 15 minutes. Cut off top quarter of pita breads and open to form pockets. Line each with lettuce leaves. Spoon about ½ cup filling into each pita bread and top with cheese.

Makes 8 servings

Serving Suggestion: Serve with vegetable sticks and fresh fruit.

Campbell's® Cheesy Broccoli

1 can (10¾ ounces) CAMPBELL'S® Condensed Cheddar
    Cheese Soup
¼ cup milk
4 cups frozen broccoli cuts

1. In 2-quart microwave-safe casserole mix soup and milk. Add broccoli.

2. Cover and microwave on HIGH 8 minutes or until broccoli is tender-crisp, stirring once during heating.   *Makes 4 servings*

Prep/Cook Time: 10 minutes

Amigo Pita Pocket Sandwiches

Cowboy Burgers

1 pound ground beef
½ teaspoon LAWRY'S® Seasoned Salt
½ teaspoon LAWRY'S® Seasoned Pepper
2 tablespoons plus 2 teaspoons butter OR
    margarine
1 large onion, thinly sliced
1 package (1.0 ounces) LAWRY'S® Taco Spices
    & Seasonings
4 slices cheddar cheese
4 Kaiser rolls
  Lettuce leaves
  Tomato slices

In medium bowl, combine ground beef, Seasoned Salt and Seasoned Pepper; shape into four patties. Grill or broil to desired doneness (about 5 to 6 minutes on each side for medium). Meanwhile, in medium skillet, melt butter. Add onion and Taco Spices & Seasonings; mix well. Cook onion over medium-high heat until soft and transparent. Top each patty with onions and cheese. Return to grill or broiler until cheese is melted. Place each patty on roll; top with lettuce and tomato.   *Makes 4 servings*

Serving Suggestion: Serve with baked beans.

Cowboy Burger

Tic-Tac-Toe Tuna Pizza

1 bread-style prepared pizza crust (10 ounces)
1 can (12 ounces) tuna packed in water, drained
½ cup minced onion
⅓ cup reduced-fat mayonnaise
9 thin plum tomato slices
4 to 5 slices (¾ ounce each) process cheese
    food or American cheese

1. Preheat oven to 425°F. Place pizza crust on pizza pan or baking sheet.

2. Combine tuna, onion and mayonnaise in medium bowl; season to taste with salt and pepper. Stir until blended. Spread mixture over crust, leaving 1-inch border. Arrange tomato slices on tuna mixture in 3 rows, spacing at least ½ inch apart.

3. Bake 10 to 12 minutes or until heated through.

4. While pizza is baking, cut cheese slices into ½-inch-wide strips.

5. Remove pizza from oven. Arrange enough strips over tuna mixture to resemble tic-tac-toe game. Crisscross remaining strips over some tomato slices. Let stand 5 minutes before serving.

Makes 6 servings

Prep and Cook Time: 30 minutes

Tic-Tac-Toe Tuna Pizza

Hearty BBQ Beef Sandwiches

1 envelope LIPTON® RECIPE SECRETS® Onion
    Soup Mix
2 cups water
½ cup chili sauce
¼ cup firmly packed light brown sugar
1 (3-pound) boneless chuck roast
8 kaiser rolls or hamburger buns, toasted

1. Preheat oven to 325°F. In Dutch oven or 5-quart heavy ovenproof saucepot, combine soup mix, water, chili sauce and sugar; add roast.

2. Cover and bake 3 hours or until roast is tender.

3. Remove roast; reserve juices. Bring reserved juices to a boil over high heat. Boil 4 minutes.

4. Meanwhile, with fork, shred roast. Stir roast into reserved juices and simmer, stirring frequently, 1 minute. Serve on rolls.

Makes 8 servings

Recipe Tip: Always measure brown sugar in a dry measure cup and pack down firmly. To soften hardened brown sugar, place in glass dish with 1 slice of bread. Cover with plastic wrap and microwave at HIGH 30 to 40 seconds. Let stand 30 seconds; stir. Remove bread.

Hearty BBQ Beef Sandwich

Sweet Treats

Sugar and spice and everything nice! That's what these yummy goodies are made of. Scrumptious cookies, cupcakes and desserts will tempt anyone who has eaten all their vegetables.

Dish of Dirt

14 OREO® Chocolate Sandwich Cookies, finely crushed (about 1 cup crumbs), divided
1 pint chocolate ice cream
¼ cup chocolate-flavored syrup
Gummy worms, for garnish
Prepared whipped topping, for garnish

In each of 4 dessert dishes, place 2 tablespoons cookie crumbs. Top each with ½ cup ice cream, remaining 2 tablespoons cookie crumbs and 1 tablespoon syrup. Garnish with gummy worms and whipped topping.

Makes 4 servings

Dish of Dirt

Peanut Butter and Jelly Sandwich Cookies

1 package (about 18 ounces) refrigerated sugar
   cookie dough
1 tablespoon unsweetened cocoa powder
   All-purpose flour (optional)
1¾ cups creamy peanut butter
½ cup grape jam or jelly

1. Remove dough from wrapper according to package directions. Reserve ¼ of dough; cover and refrigerate remaining ¾ of dough. Combine reserved dough and cocoa in small bowl; refrigerate.

2. Shape remaining ¾ dough into 5½-inch log. Sprinkle with flour to minimize sticking, if necessary. Remove chocolate dough from refrigerator; roll on sheet of waxed paper to 9½×6½-inch rectangle. Place dough log in center of rectangle.

3. Bring waxed paper edges and chocolate dough up and together over log. Press gently on top and sides of dough so entire log is wrapped in chocolate dough. Flatten log slightly to form square. Wrap in waxed paper. Freeze 10 minutes.

4. Preheat oven to 350°F. Remove waxed paper from dough. Cut dough into ¼-inch slices. Place slices 2 inches apart on ungreased cookie sheets. Reshape dough edges into square, if necessary. Press dough slightly to form indentation so dough resembles slice of bread.

5. Bake 8 to 11 minutes or until lightly browned. Remove from oven and straighten cookie edges with spatula. Cool 2 minutes on cookie sheets. Remove to wire racks; cool completely.

6. To make sandwich, spread about 1 tablespoon peanut butter on underside of 1 cookie. Spread about ½ tablespoon jam over peanut butter; top with second cookie, pressing gently. Repeat with remaining cookies.
                                        Makes 11 sandwich cookies

Peanut Butter and Jelly Sandwich Cookies

Ice Cream Cone Cakes

1 package (18¼ ounces) devil's food cake mix
plus ingredients to prepare mix
⅓ cup sour cream
1 package flat-bottomed ice cream cones (about
18 cones)
1¼ cups nonfat frozen yogurt (any flavor)
Cake decorations or chocolate sprinkles

1. Preheat oven to 350°F. Grease and flour 8- or 9-inch round cake pan; set aside.

2. Prepare cake mix according to package directions, substituting sour cream for ⅓ cup of the water and decreasing oil to ¼ cup.

3. Spoon ½ of the batter (about 2⅓ cups) evenly into ice cream cones, using about 2 tablespoons batter for each. Pour remaining batter into prepared cake pan.

4. Stand cones on cookie sheet. Bake cones and cake layer until toothpick inserted into center of cake comes out clean, about 20 minutes for cones and about 35 minutes for cake layer. Cool on wire racks, removing cake from pan after 10 minutes. Reserve or freeze cake layer for another use.

5. Top each filled cone with ¼ cup scoop of frozen yogurt just before serving. Sprinkle with decorations as desired. Serve immediately.

Makes 18 servings

Ice Cream Cone Cakes

Wild Side Sundaes

4 packages (4-serving size) JELL-O® Brand
    Gelatin, 4 different flavors
4 cups boiling water
2 cups cold water
1 tub (8 ounces) COOL WHIP® Whipped
    Topping, thawed
    Additional thawed COOL WHIP® Whipped
    Topping

DISSOLVE each package of gelatin completely in 1 cup boiling water in separate bowls. Stir ½ cup cold water into each bowl of gelatin. Pour each mixture into separate 8-inch square pans. Refrigerate at least 3 hours or until firm. Cut gelatin in each pan into ½-inch cubes.

LAYER gelatin cubes alternately with whipped topping in sundae glasses. Garnish with dollop of additional whipped topping.

REFRIGERATE until ready to serve.   *Makes 16 servings*

Wild Side Sundaes

Cookies & Cream Cupcakes

2¼ cups all-purpose flour
1 tablespoon baking powder
½ teaspoon salt
1⅔ cups sugar
1 cup milk
½ cup butter, softened
2 teaspoons vanilla
3 egg whites
1 cup crushed chocolate sandwich cookies
   (about 10 cookies) plus additional for
   garnish
1 (16-ounce) container prepared vanilla frosting

1. Preheat oven to 350°F. Line 24 regular-size (2½-inch) muffin pan cups with paper muffin cup liners.

2. Sift flour, baking powder and salt together in large bowl. Stir in sugar. Add milk, butter and vanilla; beat with electric mixer at low speed 30 seconds. Beat at medium speed 2 minutes. Add egg whites; beat 2 minutes. Stir in 1 cup crushed cookies.

3. Spoon batter into prepared muffin pans. Bake 20 to 25 minutes or until toothpick inserted into centers comes out clean. Cool in pans on wire racks 10 minutes. Remove to racks; cool completely.

4. Frost cupcakes; garnish with additional crushed cookies.

Makes 24 cupcakes

Cookies & Cream Cupcakes

Brownie Sandwich Cookies

BROWNIE COOKIES
  1 package DUNCAN HINES® Chocolate Lovers
    Double Fudge Brownie Mix
  1 egg
  3 tablespoons water
  Sugar

FILLING
  1 container (16 ounces) DUNCAN HINES®
    Creamy Homestyle Cream Cheese Frosting
  Red food coloring (optional)
  ½ cup semisweet mini chocolate chips

1. Preheat oven to 375°F. Grease cookie sheets.

2. For brownie cookies, combine brownie mix, fudge packet from mix, egg and water in large bowl. Stir until well blended, about 50 strokes. Shape dough into 50 (1-inch) balls. Place 2 inches apart on prepared cookie sheets. Grease bottom of drinking glass; dip in sugar. Press gently to flatten 1 cookie to ⅜-inch thickness. Repeat with remaining cookies. Bake at 375°F for 6 to 7 minutes or until set. Cool 1 minute on cookie sheets. Remove to cooling racks. Cool completely.

3. For filling, tint frosting with red food coloring, if desired. Stir in chocolate chips.

4. To assemble, spread 1 tablespoon frosting on bottom of one cookie; top with second cookie. Press together to make sandwich cookie. Repeat with remaining cookies.

Makes 25 sandwich cookies

Brownie Sandwich Cookies

Mud Slides

2 cups cold milk
1 package (4-serving size) JELL-O® Chocolate
  Flavor Instant Pudding & Pie Filling
14 chocolate sandwich cookies, finely crushed
  (about 1½ cups)
2 cups thawed COOL WHIP® Whipped Topping

LINE bottoms and sides of 2 loaf pans with wet paper towels. Tilt 2 (12-ounce) glasses in each pan.

POUR milk into 1-quart container with tight-fitting lid. Add pudding mix; cover tightly. Shake vigorously at least 45 seconds; pour evenly into glasses.

GENTLY stir 1¼ cups of the cookies into whipped topping with wire whisk in medium bowl until blended. Spoon evenly over pudding in glasses; sprinkle with remaining ¼ cup cookies.

REFRIGERATE until ready to serve.   *Makes 4 servings*

Mud Slide

Perfect Parties

Looking for some new ideas for your child's next party? Choose these tasty recipes to make your tyke's next birthday or celebration easy for you and memorable for them.

Campfire Hot Dogs

½ pound ground beef
2 cups RAGÚ® Old World Style® Pasta Sauce
1 can (10¾ to 16 ounces) baked beans
8 frankfurters, cooked
8 frankfurter rolls

1. In 12-inch skillet, brown ground beef over medium-high heat; drain.

2. Stir in Ragú Pasta Sauce and beans. Bring to a boil over high heat. Reduce heat to low and simmer, stirring occasionally, 5 minutes.

3. To serve, arrange frankfurters in rolls and top with sauce mixture. Garnish, if desired, with Cheddar cheese.
Makes 8 servings

Tip: For Chili Campfire Hot Dogs, simply stir 2 to 3 teaspoon chili powder into sauce mixture.

Prep Time: 5 minutes
Cook Time: 10 minutes

Campfire Hot Dogs

Octo-Dogs and Shells

4 hot dogs
1½ cups uncooked small shell pasta
1½ cups frozen mixed vegetables
1 cup prepared Alfredo sauce
Prepared yellow mustard in squeeze bottle
Cheese-flavored fish-shaped crackers

Lay 1 hot dog on side with end facing you. Starting 1 inch from one end of hot dog, slice hot dog vertically in half. Roll hot dog ¼ turn and slice in half vertically again, making 4 segments connected at the top. Slice each segment in half vertically, creating a total of 8 "legs." Repeat with remaining hot dogs.

Place hot dogs in medium saucepan; cover with water. Bring to a boil over medium-high heat. Remove from heat; set aside.

Prepare pasta according to package directions, stirring in vegetables during last 3 minutes of cooking time. Drain; return to pan. Stir in Alfredo sauce. Heat over low heat until heated through. Divide pasta mixture between four plates.

Drain "octo-dogs." Arrange one octo-dog on top of pasta mixture on each plate. Draw faces on "heads" of octo-dogs with mustard. Sprinkle crackers over pasta mixture. *Makes 4 servings*

Octo-Dog and Shells

Smushy Cookies

1 package (20 ounces) refrigerated cookie
    dough, any flavor
All-purpose flour (optional)
Peanut butter, multi-colored miniature
    marshmallows, assorted colored sprinkles,
    chocolate-covered raisins and caramel candy
    squares

1. Preheat oven to 350°F. Grease cookie sheets.

2. Remove dough from wrapper according to package directions. Cut into 4 equal sections. Reserve 1 section; refrigerate remaining 3 sections.

3. Roll reserved dough to ¼-inch thickness. Sprinkle with flour to minimize sticking, if necessary. Cut out cookies using 2½-inch round cookie cutter. Transfer to prepared cookie sheets. Repeat with remaining dough, working with 1 section at a time.

4. Bake 8 to 11 minutes or until edges are light golden brown. Remove to wire racks; cool completely.

5. To make sandwich, spread about 1½ tablespoons peanut butter on underside of 1 cookie to within ¼ inch of edge. Sprinkle with miniature marshmallows and candy pieces. Top with second cookie, pressing gently. Repeat with remaining cookies and fillings.

6. Just before serving, place sandwiches on paper towels. Microwave at HIGH 15 to 25 seconds or until fillings become soft.

Makes about 8 to 10 sandwich cookies

Smushy Cookies

Chili Chip Party Platter

1 pound ground beef
1 medium onion, chopped
1 package (1.48 ounces) LAWRY'S® Spices
    && Seasonings for Chili
1 can (6 ounces) tomato paste
1 cup water
1 bag (8 to 9 ounces) tortilla chips or corn chips
1½ cups (6 ounces) shredded cheddar cheese
1 can (2¼ ounces) sliced pitted black olives,
    drained
½ cup sliced green onions

In medium skillet, cook ground beef until browned and crumbly; drain fat. Add onion, Spices & Seasonings for Chili, tomato paste and water; mix well. Bring to a boil over medium-high heat. Reduce heat to low; simmer, uncovered, 15 minutes, stirring occasionally. Serve over tortilla chips. Top with cheddar cheese, olives and green onion.

Makes 4 servings

Serving Suggestion: Serve with a cool beverage and sliced melon.

Chili Chip Party Platter

Cinnamon RedHot® Popcorn

10 cups air-popped popcorn (½ cup unpopped)
1½ cups (7 ounces) coarsely chopped pecans
¾ cup granulated sugar
¾ cup packed light brown sugar
½ cup light corn syrup
3 tablespoons *Frank's® RedHot®* Sauce
2 tablespoons honey
6 tablespoons (¾ stick) unsalted butter, at room
    temperature, cut into thin pats
1 tablespoon ground cinnamon

1. Preheat oven to 250°F. Place popcorn and pecans in 5-quart ovenproof bowl or Dutch oven. Bake 15 minutes.

2. Combine sugars, corn syrup, **RedHot** Sauce and honey in 2-quart saucepan. Bring to a full boil over medium-high heat, stirring just until sugars dissolve. Boil about 6 to 8 minutes or until soft crack stage (290°F on candy thermometer). *Do not stir.* Remove from heat.

3. Gradually add butter and cinnamon to sugar mixture, stirring gently until well blended. Pour over popcorn, tossing to coat evenly.* Spread popcorn mixture on greased baking sheets, using two forks. Cool completely. Break into bite-size pieces. Store in airtight container up to 2 weeks.   *Makes 18 cups*

If popcorn mixture sets too quickly, return to oven to rewarm. Popcorn mixture may be shaped into 3-inch balls while warm, if desired.

Prep Time: 15 minutes
Cook Time: 8 to 10 minutes

Cinnamon RedHot* Popcorn

Dream Castle

5¼ cups Buttercream Frosting (page 60)
   Blue and yellow food color
3 (8-inch) square cakes, tops and edges trimmed
2 cups Base Frosting (page 60), optional
   Assorted colored sugar
4 sugar ice cream cones
   Small purple and white gumdrops
      Pastel candy-coated chocolate pieces
2 pink sugar wafer cookies
1 (19×13-inch) cake board, cut in half crosswise
   and covered

1. Color ½ cup Buttercream Frosting blue and ½ cup yellow; reserve 4¼ cups white frosting. Place one square cake on prepared cake board. Frost top with some of the white frosting.

2. Cut remaining cakes as shown in diagrams 1 and 2 (see page 60).

3. Place piece A over bottom layer. Frost top of piece A with some of the white frosting. Position remaining pieces as shown in diagram 3 (see page 60), connecting with some of the white frosting.

4. Frost entire cake with Base Frosting to seal in crumbs. Frost again with white frosting. Cover piece D (bridge) with colored sugar.

5. Frost cones with blue and yellow frostings. Place as shown.

6. Decorate as shown, using frosting to attach candies, if needed. Arrange wafer cookies on front of castle for gate.

Makes 24 to 28 servings

continued on page 60

Dream Castle

Dream Castle, continued

Buttercream Frosting

6 cups powdered sugar, sifted and divided
¾ cup butter or margarine, softened
¼ cup shortening
6 to 8 tablespoons milk, divided
1 teaspoon vanilla extract

Place 3 cups sugar, butter, shortening, 4 tablespoons milk and vanilla in large bowl. Beat with electric mixer until smooth. Add remaining 3 cups powdered sugar; beat at medium speed until light and fluffy, adding more milk, 1 tablespoon at a time, as needed for good spreading consistency. *Makes about 3½ cups frosting*

Base Frosting

3 cups powdered sugar, sifted
½ cup shortening
¼ cup milk plus additional, if necessary
½ teaspoon vanilla

Combine sugar, shortening, ¼ cup milk and vanilla in large bowl. Beat with electric mixer on medium speed until smooth. Add more milk, 1 teaspoon at a time, until frosting is a thin consistency. Use frosting immediately. *Makes about 2 cups*

Acknowledgments

The publishers would like to thank the companies and organizations listed below for the use of their recipes and photographs in this publication.

Bob Evans®

Campbell Soup Company

Duncan Hines® and Moist Deluxe® are registered trademarks of Aurora Foods Inc.

The Golden Grain Company®

Kraft Foods, Inc.

Lawry's® Foods, Inc.

Lipton®

OREO® Chocolate Sandwich Cookies

Reckitt Benckiser

The J. M. Smucker Company

StarKist® Seafood Company

Texas Peanut Producers Board

index

index

Metric Conversion Chart

VOLUME MEASUREMENTS (dry)

⅛ teaspoon = 0.5 mL

¼ teaspoon = 1 mL

½ teaspoon = 2 mL

¾ teaspoon = 4 mL

1 teaspoon = 5 mL

1 tablespoon = 15 mL

2 tablespoons = 30 mL

¼ cup = 60 mL

⅓ cup = 75 mL

½ cup = 125 mL

⅔ cup = 150 mL

¾ cup = 175 mL

1 cup = 250 mL

2 cups = 1 pint = 500 mL

3 cups = 750 mL

4 cups = 1 quart = 1 L

VOLUME MEASUREMENTS (fluid)

1 fluid ounce (2 tablespoons) = 30 mL

4 fluid ounces (½ cup) = 125 mL

8 fluid ounces (1 cup) = 250 mL

12 fluid ounces (1½ cups) = 375 mL

16 fluid ounces (2 cups) = 500 mL

WEIGHTS (mass)

½ ounce = 15 g

1 ounce = 30 g

3 ounces = 90 g

4 ounces = 120 g

8 ounces = 225 g

10 ounces = 285 g

12 ounces = 360 g

16 ounces = 1 pound = 450 g

DIMENSIONS

1/16 inch = 2 mm

⅛ inch = 3 mm

¼ inch = 6 mm

½ inch = 1.5 cm

¾ inch = 2 cm

1 inch = 2.5 cm

OVEN TEMPERATURES

250°F = 120°C

275°F = 140°C

300°F = 150°C

325°F = 160°C

350°F = 180°C

375°F = 190°C

400°F = 200°C

425°F = 220°C

450°F = 230°C

BAKING PAN SIZES

Utensil	Size in Inches/ Quarts	Metric Volume	Size in Centimeters
Baking or Cake Pan (square or rectangular)	8×8×2	2 L	20×20×5
	9×9×2	2.5 L	23×23×5
	12×8×2	3 L	30×20×5
	13×9×2	3.5 L	33×23×5
Loaf Pan	8×4×3	1.5 L	20×10×7
	9×5×3	2 L	23×13×7
Round Layer Cake Pan	8×1½	1.2 L	20×4
	9×1½	1.5 L	23×4
Pie Plate	8×1¼	750 mL	20×3
	9×1¼	1 L	23×3
Baking Dish or Casserole	1 quart	1 L	—
	1½ quart	1.5 L	—
	2 quart	2 L	—

Top to bottom: Reindeer Pancake, Bunny Pancake
with Strawberry Butter

Breakfast Baskets

8 (6-inch) flour tortillas, divided
4 tablespoons butter, melted and divided
4 bacon slices, cut into 1-inch pieces
½ cup chopped green bell pepper
½ cup chopped red bell pepper
3 tablespoons chopped onion
4 eggs
3 tablespoons milk
¼ teaspoon salt
¼ teaspoon hot pepper sauce (optional)
⅛ teaspoon black pepper

1. Preheat oven to 350°F.

2. Brush 6 tortillas with melted butter; let stand until pliable, about 5 minutes. Gently ease buttered tortillas into 6 small custard cups.

3. For handles, cut each of both remaining tortillas into 3 (1-inch) strips. (There should be 6 strips.) Brush with remaining butter. Invert muffin pan; arrange 2 strips in "u" shape around bottoms of each of 3 cups. Bake tortilla cups and handles 10 to 15 minutes or until golden brown. Remove cups and handles to wire rack; cool.

4. Meanwhile, cook bacon in medium skillet over medium-high heat until crisp, stirring occasionally. Remove bacon from skillet; set aside. Pour off all but 1 tablespoon bacon fat from skillet. Add bell peppers and onion to skillet; cook and stir until crisp-tender.

5. Whisk together eggs, milk, salt, hot pepper sauce and pepper. Add to vegetable mixture in skillet; cook and stir until eggs are set. Stir in bacon. Divide egg mixture evenly among prepared baskets. Place handles in baskets. Serve warm.   *Makes 6 servings*

Breakfast Pizza

Bunny Pancakes with Strawberry Butter

Strawberry Butter (recipe follows)
2 cups buttermilk baking mix
1 cup milk
2 eggs
½ cup plain yogurt
Assorted candies

1. Prepare Strawberry Butter; set aside. Preheat electric skillet or griddle to 375°F.

2. Combine baking mix, milk, eggs and yogurt in medium bowl; mix well. Spoon scant ½ cup batter into skillet. With back of spoon, gently spread batter into 4-inch circle. Spoon about 2 tablespoons batter onto top edge of circle for head. Using back of spoon, spread batter from head to form bunny ears as shown in photo.

3. Cook until bubbles on surface begin to pop and top of pancake appears dry; turn pancake over. Cook until done, 1 to 2 minutes. Decorate with candies as shown in photo.

4. Repeat with remaining batter. Serve warm with Strawberry Butter.
Makes about 12 (8-inch) pancakes

Strawberry Butter: Place 1 package (3 ounces) cream cheese and ½ cup softened butter in food processor or blender; process until smooth. Add ⅓ cup sugar; process until combined. Add 1½ cups fresh or thawed frozen strawberries; process until finely chopped.

Reindeer Pancakes: Prepare batter as directed. Spoon scant ¼ cup batter into skillet. Quickly spread batter with back of spoon to form antlers as shown in photo. Cook as directed. Decorate as shown in photo. Serve as directed.